GOD IS YOUR PARTNER

John-Roger, D.S.S.

OTHER BOOKS BY JOHN-ROGER

Blessings of Light

The Consciousness of Soul

Divine Essence

Dream Voyages

*Forgiveness—
the Key to the Kingdom*

Fulfilling Your Spiritual Promise

Inner Worlds of Meditation

The Journey of a Soul

Living Love from the Spiritual Heart

Loving Each Day

*Loving Each Day
for Moms & Dads*

Loving Each Day for Peacemakers

Manual on Using the Light

*Momentum:
Letting Love Lead
(with Paul Kaye)*

Passage Into Spirit

The Path to Mastership

The Power Within You

Psychic Protection

*Relationships:
Love, Marriage and Spirit*

Sex, Spirit and You

The Spiritual Family

*Spiritual High
(with Michael McBay)*

The Spiritual Promise

*Spiritual Warrior:
The Art of Spiritual Living*

The Tao of Spirit

Walking with the Lord

The Way Out Book

Wealth & Higher Consciousness

*What's It Like Being You?
(with Paul Kaye)*

*When Are You Coming Home?
(with Pauli Sanderson)*

GOD IS YOUR PARTNER

John-Roger, D.S.S.

Mandeville Press
Los Angeles, California

Mandeville Press
P.O. Box 513935
Los Angeles, California 90051-1935
(323) 737-4055
jrbooks@mandevillepress.org
www.mandevillepress.org

Printed in China
ISBN 978-1893020-26-9

TABLE OF CONTENTS

Tithing and seeding,

done with the right attitude of giving,

can open your Spirit and bring you to

an inner peace inside, by balancing some of

the karmic blocks that have stood in your way.

And if, on top of that, you get the material things,

you're getting your cake and eating it, too.

FOREWORD

*Seeding and Tithing are the
left and right hands of God.*

There is a story told of a soul whose time has finally come to enter into the world for what it hopes will be the last time. The Soul goes before the karmic board, which is the group that helps a Soul decide its life plan. The board looks at the Soul and says, "We have a very good life for you. In this life you are going to find someone who can take you back to God, and you will be able to lift from this world and go back to your true home in Spirit."

The Soul says, "Fantastic!"

The karmic board asks, "What is it worth to you?" and the Soul says, "To get off the planet? To go back to God? It's worth everything! I'll give it all!"

The karmic board looks at the Soul and says, "That's not necessary. All you need to do is give 10 percent."

The Soul says, "Ten percent? Last time I was on Earth, that's what I gave my agent. That's nothing!"

"Well," the karmic board says, "if you do give the 10 percent, you will be filled with so many blessings that you will not have room enough to receive all of them."

The Soul says, "Incredible! I give 10 percent, I find a spiritual teacher, I get tons of blessings, and I go back to God. What a deal! There must be a catch."

There's a moment of silence, and one of the elders on the karmic board looks at the Soul and says, "Yes, there is a catch. When you get down there, you won't want to do it."

So here we are on our way home to God, and many of us are saying, "I really don't want to tithe or seed."

Seeding and tithing are not requirements for participation in MSIA. In fact, as of the time of this writing, most people in MSIA don't tithe or seed. But the people who do are blessed with many gifts. It's a beautiful thing to do.

The financial level is the smallest part of this whole process. The biggest part is to open to the blessings of Spirit in your life and to know God in a greater way. And who could wish for a greater gift than to know God?

Paul Kaye

TITHING

Tithing is about placing God first in your life.
Being a joyful giver is a great part of loving the Lord
with your body, mind, and Soul.

For our time, tithing goes back

to the time of Abraham

when he gave to the high priest, Melchizedek.

But when Jesus came in and incarnated,

the old law of tithing was superseded

by a new process under the Christ.

So we take the old law and move it around

to realign it with the new energy flow.

When you tithe to MSIA, you tithe in that

new energy flow under the Christ.

That means when you tithe

out of your goodness and gratitude,

there is going to be a lot of grace

coming your way.

1

ORIGINS OF TITHING

Then Melchizedek king of Salem brought out bread and wine. He was priest of God Most High, and he blessed Abram... Then Abram gave him a tenth of everything.   *(Genesis 14:18–20 NIV)*

When the prophet Abram (later Abraham) was traveling home with the riches of battle after warring with a nearby king, he was met by a high priest in the order of God. This priest was Melchizedek, and it was at that time that the Priesthood of Melchizedek was established on the planet. Melchizedek was a direct radiation or emanation of the man who later came and was known as Jesus Christ.

The high priest in the order of God is Christ and is also referred to as the Messiah. As soon as Abraham saw Melchizedek, the wisdom of his heart knew he was seeing one who is with God. Abraham knew intuitively that he was to give back 10 percent of all that he had in the world to the representative of God, and so began the practice of tithing. Melchizedek occupied the office of the Christ, as did some other prophets of the Old Testament. However, no one until the time of Jesus had the office of the Christ totally in one place at one time. When it is said that Christ is the only begotten Son of God, it means that God created one Soul energy and it went into all people. This means that we all have the elements of Christ within us.

When Abraham was blessed and then gave Melchizedek a tenth of everything, a spiritual covenant was set up for our time, whereby humankind is to give a tenth of its increase (what a person receives that is his or hers) back to God.

The above passage from the Bible may not sound like a covenant. But what it's not saying here is that there were hundreds of people around, and there was merry-making, singing, praising, and hosannas. And there was all this booty laid out from the war Abraham had won.

The image you can get from the Bible is that two people met on a rock and shook hands. But it wasn't like that. This was flesh and blood, and when you put flesh and blood on the situation, you get that this was a major occurrence, an epic event.

As humankind fulfills its part of the covenant by giving 10 percent to God, then God fulfills his part by continually blessing us. God, of course, is always fulfilling his part anyway, so the question is, are we lining up, are we fulfilling the covenant?

People sometimes resist this process of giving their tithe. Interestingly, it doesn't belong to you in the first place; you are just restoring it to its rightful owner—God. Historically, people have tended to trust in materiality for their success. Instead of trusting in the Lord for their success, they trust in money or riches. Therefore, they withhold their tithes so they can have a lot more they can trust.

This happened to the ancient Hebrews, who, instead of being a pleasure to the Lord, sometimes turned to their own pleasures and stopped tithing. It wasn't too long before things went awry. When they questioned why, the answer was always that they had forsaken or given up on the Lord and that they had broken God's covenant. Then the people would restore the covenant by tithing; they would start to flourish again, and there would be no war.

Our job is to overcome our lower nature so we can live in the awareness of our Soul. When we tithe to the church or God, we are making the material world let go of us. So tithing is also part of a spiritual law and assists us in getting free of materialistic confinement.

In Malachi, it is asked, *"Will a man rob God? Yet you rob me... in tithes and offerings" (Malachi 3:8 NIV)*. The question is, can God be robbed? No, but his covenant can be broken, and that is robbing God of the covenant. Later on in the same chapter, it is said, *"Bring the whole tithe into the storehouse... Test me in this... and see if I will not throw open the floodgates of heaven and pour out so much blessing that you will not have room enough for it." (Malachi 8:10 NIV)*.

When a person tithes, the universe that works under the spiritual law of tithing says, "If you have that much to give, that means you are open to receive more." In biblical times, people who tithed often received one hundredfold more than what they had given. When they received their hundredfold, they then gave 10 percent of that.

In MSIA many people know about the principle of tithing through my book, *Wealth and Higher Consciousness*. The book says that when we give to ourselves first, we tithe to the Christ within. Then, if we want to give to the church, we do that. If we want to build an organization, we tithe to the organization, and because we are part of the organization, we also get to receive of its wealth.

So, you may want to check it out with a joyful attitude of saying, "Lord, I am open to receive whatever it is that you bless me with." And then discover for yourself the blessing of fulfilling God's covenant.

God said,

"Ten percent of everything
you own comes to me first.
Any increase you get,
I get 10 percent first.
That's mine."

What He really should have said is
"It's all mine and you can have 90 percent."

Spirit said to me,

"You have to give it all."

So I gave it all.

From that day, the Church became one of

the wealthier churches around for its size.

My attitude was God first,

Jesus second, and myself third.

That made up the Triune of God.

From that point on, whomever I worked with—

large corporations, individuals, any kind of group—

they prospered because God is my Partner.

And wherever I went to work, God went with me.

God doesn't know failure.

LETTING GO

"Bring the whole tithe into the storehouse, that there may be food in my house. Test me in this," says the Lord Almighty, "and see if I will not throw open the floodgates of heaven and pour out so much blessing that you will not have room enough for it." (Malachi 3:10 NIV)

One of the fundamental errors that we have as human beings is greed, which is manifested mostly in terms of money or monetary value. Greed, by its very nature, is a striking against the riches within oneself because it appears that there is never enough here in the world. Our eyes are always "hungry."

We can help to break the greed pattern by tithing, giving 10 percent of our personal wealth. When we tithe, two levels are activated—a level here in this world and, at the same time, a mystical, invisible level. The mystical is a communication saying, "You are abundant and handle abundance well, so here's some more." The other level, in this world, is when we look at our abundance and contribute joyfully through tithing. We are actually cheerful about it. This action sets up a countenance that is a form of glory in the human being, and that glory attracts more abundance.

When one person becomes free of materiality, it's like an infection going the other way. Instead of greed affecting honest people, honest people start affecting the greedy. You let go and give to God, joyfully and unconditionally. With people who say, "I don't have enough to tithe," I say, "Don't tithe," because their feelings of lack are telling them that they're going to need it. And with that attitude, they won't have enough anyway. Because they're hanging on, God can't supply them with more. They're holding on to it, scared to death about letting go of it. However, if they let go, they can rise to new heights inside themselves and get freer.

It's simple to tithe: you just give back 10 percent of what you earn to the source of your spiritual teachings. To those working with the Traveler Consciousness, this would be the Movement of Spiritual Inner Awareness. MSIA is a tax-exempt church, but tithing isn't done in terms of a tax deduction. It's done for the joy of giving. When you lovingly donate in this way, the abundance starts to come to you in many ways.

Tithing is actually a spiritual law: to give back to the source of your spiritual teachings. When you commit to doing it, something inside you works differently from that day forward.

Conditions may or may not immediately change in the physical, but inside, it can work wonders. And you finally own the Movement of Spiritual Inner Awareness. Before, it may have seemed like you couldn't really own it, like it was someplace in California, Chicago, or New York. When you tithe, you realize that it's right here. Wherever you are, that's the center.

I tell people, try it. Test it to see if it's true or not. Almost everybody who tithes keeps tithing because they say it works. The Bible says to tithe, to try God, and he'll pour blessings upon you. Some people think, "If I tithe, I'll get lots of money." That isn't what was said. It was said that God will pour blessings upon you. You may suddenly lose your headaches, or a backache may disappear. Or you may find that your spouse is getting along real well with you, or that the plumbing that was always getting stuck is no longer stuck, or that the person at the bank who was always hassling you has been transferred. These little miracles of perfect timing take place, and you say, "I can't believe this is all due to tithing." And I just tell people, "You have to check it out in order to know for yourself." I know for me.

I know people who tithe a lot

and some who try to get out of it.

You don't have to tithe anything.

But if you're going to tithe,

first and foremost you've got to be cheerful about it,

and then you've got to be grateful

and thankful about it, and finally,

you've got to be honest inside of you about it.

There's a trust that you're doing

what is right and proper for you.

3

IS TITHING BUYING OFF GOD?

Q: When I tithe, it feels really good. It just feels wonderful when I write the checks. However, when I attend a tithing evening or I talk about it with others, it feels like somehow I'm attempting to buy God off.

A: In a sense, you really are. But you're not buying off some cosmic God. You're really addressing the God inside of yourself. It works almost the same way as doing things for your basic self, to get it to cooperate and to assist it in coming into line.

When you tithe, it is actually God buying you off, where God is the center of the universe bringing you into alignment by the process of tithing.

If you speak from your ego-center, saying, "I'm buying God off," it's absolutely a farce, it's ridiculous, and it cannot be done. That's like buying the air off. The air buys you off by giving itself to you.

Now, the negative power, which I suspect may put a word in your ear, will say, "This scam, this scheme, this conniving is just an attempt to get money from the people in a dishonest way, an unsatisfactory way, an underhanded way." The negative power has a lot of ways that it tries to do this. And usually it'll say, "And I don't have enough money to tithe. The kid needs shoes. I need this, I need that, I need this." And it turns you back to your materiality.

You can always tell when the negative power is doing that because it turns you to your lack. "How will I have the money to fly the plane to go do my spiritual work?" If you stop for a minute and look neutrally, you will realize that you put the material before the spiritual because spiritual work can be done anywhere. So it's important that you watch the trickiness of the negative power because it can use your mind and emotions.

If the negative power came in with a pitchfork and a long tail and a red outfit, you'd go, "Aha! I know you. Get out of here!" But it comes in a most reasonable and well-mannered way. And its argument is your own argument, so it can very easily convince you or tempt you to your failure. To overcome it is simple. The real key is the joyfulness and the essence behind the giving.

The essence is so important. The tithe is recorded, but no one can record the essence, which to me is where I live and where I would like you to live because all that materiality goes by the wayside some way or another. It goes. But the essence is always present if we want to turn toward it.

It's very true that if you tithe you know God,

but it is also true that if you want to know God, you tithe.

The statement works both ways.

The basic principle of abundance
is that you tithe on the "first fruits of the harvest."
If you're not, then you are thwarting yourself
of receiving the abundance that comes from tithing.

Some people say, "I don't have enough money
to meet my bills, let alone tithe."
That may be very true, and
it may be like that all their life
because they do not have God as their partner.
They have themselves as a selfish partner.

TITHING:

A UNIVERSAL LAW

As human beings, we have a challenge about materialism and spirituality. It's a really big challenge, but there is a way to combat materialism that's very simple. It's the law of tithing. If I gave you a car to drive today, would you give it back to me at the end of the day? Yes, because it's not yours. Even if you drove it all day and put gas in it, it's not yours. Tithing is almost a parallel to that example.

The hardest addiction on the planet to break is the self-possessiveness of "I own—I own this, I own that. And what I work for, I own." But it's not really ours, because the bounty is the Lord's and the fullness thereof. But what is of the earth belongs to the negative power. From the Soul realm down is the negative. And I wouldn't be praying to the Lord of the planet for hell or high water. I probably would pray to him for no hell or no high water, because that's his domain.

So, when you tithe, it's important to realize that the tithing is really a symbolic act, a gesturing of the Spirit out. By giving in this way, you are acknowledging that there is a greater something inside of you, and you begin to break the self-possessive addiction. It is that greater part that blesses you and protects you, so that "the slings and arrows of outrageous fortune" never really touch you. They may touch your personality and your mind and emotions, and if you are invested in those you are going to get hurt. But if you fall back within the Soul consciousness, the I am, they fall real short.

Many people have the attitude toward money of, "I worked for it, I earned it, it's mine." And yet if we say, "With this that has been given to me, I will give back 10 percent," we take away the "my" approach. In the giving back to the Spirit Source of what we earn, the attitude of "me, what about me?" goes away. Now, that really goes against the teachings of the negative power.

People ask if tithing is a universal law. The answer is yes, and it's one that works through the universe of Spirit, also. It works in nature, too, in a very simple way. When the trees lose their leaves, they are giving back to the Spirit. The leaves go into the ground and become a form of fertilizer.

And then the rain takes the fertilizer to the roots, and the tree grows stronger. It's a very simple thing, and it is natural law.

There is also spiritual law, which is man giving back to God. But man doesn't know where God is, so the law is to give to the Source from which you receive your spiritual teachings. It says in the Bible that anyone who receives instruction in the Word must give all good things to his instructor. How much do you give to your instructor or teacher? You give them 10 percent of all things. That's if you're taught in the Word. If you're not taught in the Word, then you can decide out of your own spirit what you give. But where you're being fed is where you tithe. So you sow to the teacher of the Word, and you reap from that teacher. And with the blessings of tithing, God gives more back again.

If we look at the universe as nonpersonal, it sees you give 10 percent, and it sees the emptiness created by your giving. Since the universe can't have emptiness in it, it fills the empty space. That is the return. If it keeps seeing the emptiness there, instead of just giving 10 percent back, it starts to give much more, until it flows over. And that is what is promised in the Bible. (*"I will ...pour out so much blessing that you will not have room enough for it." Malachi 3:10 NIV*) God has kept his word. People who tithe in MSIA experience incredible things. They don't necessarily experience money things, but they experience a freedom of the Spirit in them. It's like it's no longer in bondage.

God knows the intent of the heart. So if somebody tithes with an intent of just being a joyful giver, they may receive of the abundance. Someone who tithes without that intent may not receive because they may be concerned about where the money goes and how it's being used. It may look like they are caring, but they are not; they are being a nuisance. Because the one who tithes lets go and says, "You are the caretaker, and if you don't take care of it, God will deal with you, not me. I've kept my covenant with God."

So, your part is to give joyfully and freely. You do not look for a return, because then you are tempting God. You don't get Him into a bargain. God does not negotiate. His law is forever. His law is that of loving and giving, and He will not compromise that. [He gives what He gives, not necessarily what you want or asked for.] You must fulfill the regulations: get the tithe in the mail. Once God gets it, he gives you the return, but you must do your part first. He tells you the law, and then you start it. But, in a way, God started it first because he gave us everything, in abundance.

The true Joyful Givers

can ask God from their heart

to send healing to the world.

They have the contact with Spirit,

for these are the ones

who are amassing themselves on God's side

through tithing as a demonstration.

I know that tithing works.

The people who try it and do it with a willing heart

receive so much because God loves a joyful giver.

At first, I had a hard time being joyful with what I was giving

because I wasn't giving 100 percent.

Then those who work spiritually with me said, "Fake it."

No, they actually said, "Act like it. Act joyful."

And as I started acting joyful, joy appeared.

As I started acting wealthy, wealth appeared.

When I started giving money away to the poor people,

that showed I had abundance, and more abundance appeared.

Now the organizations that I work with are worldwide,

and they have a great deal of influence

but not because of me.

It is because God is my partner. Is God your Partner?

If the answer is "yes," then you don't have any problems.

5

Two Tithing Stories

Getting in the Game

It all began about 1½ years ago. I was stuck in a familiar pattern. No job, no car, no money. So I turned to God and yelled, "Help!"

I figured maybe I should try the PTS Abundance Class once again. I got on the bus and rode it about two hours to go to the class. I decided I was going to approach the class with a new attitude. The one I'd had was, "Oh yeah. Everything works in MSIA, except for this class and tithing and seeding."

I started to seed. It seemed to work with little things. My car got fixed. I got back on the road. I read the quotes from the class. I did a gratitude journal. I started to feel a little more positive, a little more trusting in God and this process. Little bits of money started to come in.

In the class we talked about having a clear intention. I knew what I wanted, but I'd never written it down. So I did that. I also started to keep track of my seeds, making them more specific. That seemed to work. Then came the big challenge. Tithing.

Of course, the first thought I had was "I can't afford 10 percent." I started to feel very angry, excluded, etc. Then someone in class told us that they had started to tithe 1 percent. They said that they felt that, at least that, way they were "in the game." Something inside me really heard that, so that's where I started—at 1 percent. If I had $100, all I had to tithe was $1. That I could handle. I felt like I did as a child putting money in the collection basket at church—thrilled to be participating.

Then the miracle really began to happen. I had a part-time job delivering posters, flyers, and coupons for theater events around town. It paid about $50–$100/week, and I hated it. I'd been doing it for four years, and my route was dying a slow death. I felt guilty that I wasn't giving it my all. I was burned out. Then one week I was given coupons to distribute for a show at a big theater. I really hated doing that. I trudged forward anyway. Then I realized that this did not have to be hard. I decided to use a sales technique I knew, but had not been practicing. I "assumed the sale" (very similar to "acting as if"). I called on many major stores and told them I had some special, promotional coupons for them. I saw the job differently, so they saw me in the job differently.

Three days later, the man that I worked for called me and said, "What did you do? They have redeemed almost $1 million in the past three days. This has never happened with these coupons before." To make a long story short, the show was extended for almost four months, so all those actors had jobs, and the man that I worked for saw his business really come back to life, and he paid me another $3,000 to deliver these coupons over the next six weeks (which only took me a total of, maybe, 30 hours).

During this same time, my current business began to take form. I had another part-time job packing and shipping small things for a company. Their large shipments were handled by a big company who mishandled them, and I'd have to fix the mistakes. I started doing this part-time in a friend's garage. Now, I have my own company that does all the shipments, a warehouse, and several employees, and it is expanding to possibly take on other clients.

So, what's the point of all this? Tithing and seeding do work. I have been increasing the percentage that I tithe each month. It's interesting. As I raise the percentage, Spirit seems to participate with me more. More work comes in, and more opportunities come in.

Tithing has become an investment for me. What I really want to say to those of you who don't tithe and want to is, "Start where you are. If it's just a dollar a week, do it, because you'll feel like you're participating." I've gotten so much from the teachings of MSIA that I've always wanted to be able to give back something financially. When we tithe, we really are being of service because we can make the teaching available in more ways to more people. By making the teachings available, we can feed thousands of people spiritually. Just by writing that tithing check (no matter how much it's for), we can all really be a part of it.

K.M.

Dear John-Roger,

I am writing to share with you and my fellow ministers, initiates, and Discourse subscribers about what my family has experienced since we began tithing.

Two years ago we were broke. We'd been living in a rent-controlled house for eight years and were suddenly evicted, leaving us (myself, my wife, and our seven children) faced with finding a new home. Rents had gone way up, and we had been just scraping by before. We felt desperate.

There seemed to be no solution. No one wanted to rent to a family with so many kids at any price, so in desperation I said to my wife, "Let's start tithing. We're not able to meet our financial obligations anyway." Our phone had been shut off at least ten times in the previous two years for nonpayment, and I don't even know how many collection agencies were after us.

Anyway, we started tithing and, to make a long story short, miracle after miracle started to take place for us. And, less than two years later, we are living in a beautiful home (which we now own), and my wife has a new business that gives her more money and allows her more time off.

Before we started tithing, we owed thousands of dollars. Now we are free of debt and well in the black. I just felt it was important to let people know that tithing works.

B.Mc.

Tithing is a way of saying,

"God, pour forth whatever blessing You have for me."

God is health, or lack of disease.

God is always at ease, always present, always now,

and is constantly creating and expanding.

How do you know your tithing works?

By the results that it's bearing.

And what if it doesn't bear the results?

You didn't do it out of your heart.

God says that He loves a joyful giver.

You forgot to smile as you wrote the check.

You forgot to say, "Thank you, Lord, and there's more coming.

And thanks for the health and thanks for this and this and this."

The thankfulness is like a litany,

almost like chanting the spiritual exercise mantra.

It will start to produce changes in us that are remarkable.

And often it also produces changes in other people

around us that are equally as remarkable,

because with those we love and care for,

we share the goodness and the bounty of our spirit.

6

QUESTIONS AND ANSWERS
ON TITHING

Why should I tithe?

There are no shoulds to tithing. You may, however, wish to open up a channel of greater abundance for yourself, and tithing is an effective and proven way of doing this. The abundance comes through Spirit and takes many forms. Remember, you are tithing for you, for your own growth and upliftment.

Why do you suggest I tithe to MSIA?

If you actively study Soul Awareness Discourses, MSIA is likely to be the source of your spiritual teachings. In giving to MSIA, you are, essentially, giving to yourself because you are part of it. MSIA then gives back to you through the dissemination of spiritual teachings and through having physical locations, such as Peace Awareness Labyrinth & Gardens and Windermere, where you can go for spiritual renewal.

I am on discourses, and I am studying toward initiation. I also go to church, which I often find inspiring. Can I give 5 percent to my church and 5 percent to MSIA?

A person will usually have one source for their spiritual teachings. What seems like another source is often a form of fellowship or support. Therefore, we recommend that you decide what your source is and give the full tithe to that.

I'm confused. Do I tithe on the money I receive net (after taxes) or gross (before taxes)? It seems like I've heard of both being done.

When you tithe to yourself, you tithe on the net amount of money you receive. When you tithe to the source of your spiritual teachings, you tithe on the gross (before taking out taxes), the idea being that you give to God before you give to the tax collector.

Is tithing tax-deductible?

Although MSIA is a tax-exempt organization and tithing qualifies as a contribution, many people have decided not to claim their tithes as tax deductions. This is because the money they tithe does not belong to them in the first place; it is God's, and they prefer to have their blessings come through grace rather than have the reward come through a tax deduction. Of course, it is up to you to decide what you want to do, since tithing is a matter between you and God.

I received a car as a birthday present. Someone mentioned that I needed to tithe on the value of the car. I don't think this is correct since I didn't receive any money. Am I right?

No, you are not correct. You tithe on your increase (anything that is added to you). This means that you tithe not only on money but also on the value of gifts you receive. This does not include loans, since this is not an increase because you owe the money. However, if the loan is forgiven, you would tithe on the forgiven portion.

You mean that if I receive a shirt as a gift, I tithe the value of that?

Yes, since the shirt is your increase. The attitude here is one of gratitude for the gift. People who have really lined up with tithing find that the blessings line up right behind them.

I stopped tithing and have found myself living in lack, and now I want to tithe again. Is there anything I have to do to renew my commitment?

The commitment or covenant is between you and God, so the act of tithing renews the covenant automatically. Because of the sacredness of this covenant, it is important to bring yourself back into the flow of tithing by tithing from the time you chose to start tithing again up to the time you actually send in the tithe. For example, if you recommit to tithing on March 15 and send in your first tithe on July 1, you would make sure you have tithed on all your increase from March 15 to July 1.

Is it okay to miss a tithe? I sometimes get insecure about the large bills I have to pay.

Let's look at it this way: By tithing, you have set up a channel for God's abundance. This abundance comes through in Spirit's timing. Why not keep this channel of blessings continuously open? Your tithing is your statement that you are open to receive. Tithing works from inside you, so you may want to sacrifice your insecurity for the joy that comes with giving. As Jesus said, *"The harvest is plentiful, but the laborers are few."* (Luke 10:2 RSV)

Do you suggest making tithing a lifelong habit?

Yes. Tithing is easier when it is done regularly upon receipt of income. An attitude of gratitude will usually come present as 10 percent is given to Spirit. As regular tithers have found, the blessings do pour forward, even in the testing times. This demonstrates that Spirit keeps its promise to us for life; all we are doing is choosing back.

My husband recently lost his job, and we are short of funds. Shall we tithe?

Yes. Tithing has to do with your personal relationship with God. Tithing with the correct attitude is an affirmation of that relationship. It has been set up for you to receive of God's abundance. There are often tests, but if you stick with it, you will probably be writing a success story for the *Tithing Times*.

I don't work, and I don't bring in any money. All the money I get is from my husband's work. And when he gives me money for the supermarket, I tithe 10 percent of that. Is that all right?

It's not really because that's not an increase to you. That's the supply for the family. If he gives you money for you, then I'd tithe on that. The money he gives you to buy food is not a personal increase. You're just acting as a steward, taking the money and buying supplies for the household.

What if he gives me money for clothing?

That would be different because that's your increase. However, if you're buying clothing for the other members of the family, that's not your increase. That's for the group's increase.

I've been tithing on my gross salary. I also get a lot of benefits from my company, like medical insurance and dental insurance. Do I tithe on that, too?

No, that's not an increase to you. It's a benefit to you. You don't get it. You can't tithe on what you don't get.

So you wouldn't consider that a gift?

No, because I haven't used the medical insurance plan or had my teeth fixed, or my car hasn't wrecked in ten years, so what's the increase?

What if I go to the doctor and I get 80 percent of the fees covered by the insurance company?

It's not an increase. You never saw it; it went to the doctor. If the insurance company paid 110 percent, you got a 10-percent increase and you would tithe on that amount.

I was in a car accident and I've been reimbursed for the medical expenses.

That's not an increase. It's matching funds that went out. If you get a loss settlement, above and beyond it, that's an increase. If you have to use that money to fix your car because of the damage from the accident, that's not an increase.

Just to be clear on the tax deductions: Say I deduct a donation to a university. Is the amount of the tax savings that I receive an increase?

No, that's not an increase because you have already tithed on the gross amount of income that you received.

So, if I go to a chiropractor and he doesn't charge me, would that be an increase?

Technically, if you receive lasting benefit from going to him and he would have charged $40 and he didn't charge you and you receive the benefit of healing and health from the chiropractic adjustment, $4 is tithed.

When I first started tithing, within three weeks to the day, all this negativity came on me and it was like, "I don't have enough money for this, and I don't have enough money for that." So I tithed a double tithe, and the next week I made precisely that amount of money.

I've never talked about double-portion tithing, but you just now brought it up. That is really creating more abundance.

Thanks to you, J-R, I knew what was going on when all the feelings of lack came up. I had the wit to recognize the negative power on me. So I went double time, and from that point on I've also been doing two hours of s.e.s with no problem.

Isn't that a great thing? You know it in yourself. Well, God bless you for doing it, because that's where the blessing sits.

Should I keep a money magnet, or should I tithe?

The optimum thing is to do both. However, if you were to do only one, I would suggest you tithe. Donations are man's law, tithing is spiritual law, and the money magnet is a law unto yourself.

Why is it that when I tithe to the money magnet, it's on my net income and when I tithe to MSIA, it's on my gross income?

The gross represents the totality of Spirit; it's what God has given to you. The net represents what you use for your own Soul development.

I'm in business for myself. On what amount do I tithe?

There are two things to look at here. First, there is your salary or what you draw from the business, and you would tithe on the gross amount of that. Then there is the profit the business makes. If you were in biblical times and you sold a horse, you would tithe on the increase, which would be the selling price of the horse less the cost of the horse. If we take that into modern times, you would probably tithe on the difference between the selling price of your goods and the cost of those goods to you. This is sometimes called the gross profit.

What if I am a lawyer?

Then you would probably tithe on your gross income.

Can I deduct overhead expenses in computing my tithe?

Technically speaking, no. However, it's up to you because you're the one tithing. I can only present the guidelines. Tithing is between you and God, and the most important thing is that you do it joyfully and unconditionally. God knows the intention of your heart. So the key is to keep things straight in your heart and you'll be fine.

What if I am given a scholarship or somebody gives me a room to stay in free of charge. Do I tithe on that?

Technically, yes, but on the value placed on it.

What if I don't have the money?

If you have no money, then obviously you can't tithe. But I know from observing people who tithe regularly and with the joyful attitude that they always have the money, and the blessings are pouring forth for them. You see, tithing is about putting God first in your life. Put God first in your life, and you can count on God doing His part. You will know in your heart what you are to do. Trust that and don't hassle yourself.

I tithe and I give just because, to me, that 10 percent is God's. I just write out my check, and I don't think about being joyful or anything else because that's God's, and there's not too much to think about. Is that being a joyful giver?

Yes. Joyful giving isn't doing, "Yay, team! Cheer, cheer, cheer! Fight for the Lord until you die. Rah, rah, rah!" It is the essence of what is in your heart that counts.

I have a friend who has been going through a hard time and has had difficulty earning money, and she says that every effort to do things in the world has been thwarted these past three years or so. When I suggest tithing or seeding, she says she doesn't want to, and she gives me examples of people who have not seeded or tithed and who are doing fine.

It really is too bad that she doesn't know of the God that comes to those who tithe.

I have a sense that tithing somehow keeps me more alive inside. Can you say anything about that?

Tithing is a spiritual law. You give of the first fruits; you give first to God in thanks for all that comes to you. When you do this without seeking any return but openly in gratitude for what you have received, you keep yourself under God's law, or grace, rather than the law of the negative realms. It is one way of keeping your eyes on the Lord.

You give your tithe as a spiritual duty, the same way you breathe. When you give without looking for results, you are giving openly. That giving is rewarded secretly. That secret rewarding may come as a flash of insight into the heart of God.

We suggest that you tithe 10 percent of

what you receive. That is the gross,

before things are taken out of your paycheck.

Many people said that was too difficult,

so Spirit said it would then meet them

if they gave 10 percent of what they took home.

In other words, Spirit made them a deal.

But Spirit would not give any further than that

because it isn't ours in the first place.

It is God's, and all we are doing

is recognizing that God is our partner

by giving Him 10 percent.

It's the spiritual law of tithing.

So the minimum is 10 percent.

People who tithe in MSIA experience incredible things.

They don't necessarily experience money things,
but they experience a freedom of the Spirit in them.

It's like it's no longer in bondage.

TITHING TESTIMONIALS

After resisting tithing for many years, I finally took the plunge over a year ago and started giving 1% a month. I am now up to 10%, and although I am earning more than I ever have before, I can assure you that the money is the least of the many blessings I have received from tithing.

P.F.

I live far better on 90 percent than I ever did on 100 percent.

D.C.

My life had been quite challenged financially these past couple of years and yet I'm just very aware how God takes care of me in so many ways. It's very clear that God is my Partner and tithing is just something I would not skip on as it has been such a source of strength to me.

C.L.

Because the experience of tithing is a very inner, sacred thing, many years ago I asked whether it was clear for people to share about it. J-R said that it was indeed a good thing and he said, "It's a spiritual action to share about tithing." Even more recently J-R has said, "I wish more people would share about tithing."

P.K.

We had a volunteer who just couldn't get tithing together—it just wasn't possible for her. She was dealing with a lot of financial stress, so I told her, "Why don't you try one percent?" She came back the next time, and said, "You know, I upped it a little, because it worked so well." And she continued with it and is now up to 10 percent. Tithing really works. It gives me such great joy and enthusiasm to write my check for tithing—it's the happiest check I ever write.

S.N.

I don't know what tithing does, or what the result has been—all I know is that it feels great to write that tithing check.

J.T.

Another way that tithing blesses somebody is that it moves them into realizing that they do have more than they need.

J.M.

The blessings pour over and around me. I could never have imagined the magnitude and it continues on. I trusted—my seed handled that. I tithed and put God before anything. I'm happy and living the sacred life I've always wanted.

D.M.

When I tithe, I don't look for a reward. The gratitude I feel inside is enough. In fact, for me it's the best reward of all—gratitude for participating in tithing and gratitude for the blessings I receive every day. I don't know where all these blessings come from. There are constant miracles and surprises.

L.M.

It is one of my greatest pleasures to send my tithe to MSIA. The bigger the check, the better I feel. My first tithing check was one of the biggest thrills of my life. It feels so good to give back. I am more open and receptive of Spirit and tithing has opened in me a joyful place of worthiness to receive.

K.S.F.

When I write my tithing check, it's as if my hand is lifted up to the heavens and is met by the hand of the Lord, to guide and protect me on my way home. Tithing paves the road ahead, so that I never walk alone, I walk with the Lord.

P.C.

When you tithe,

you join in with the other tithers in MSIA—

you join in that force field that's in touch with the

angels and all the blessings of God that are present.

It really demonstrates you're in

good standing with the Lord.

Many years ago someone said to me that tithing would allow me to get closer to God. For no other reason, I did it and have never regretted a moment. Tithing aligns me inside with the place that is already secure, full, abundant, and above and beyond the cares of the world. It allows me, quite magically, to let go and let God.

K.W.

Tithing to me has been a life line to God. Over the years my husband and I have experienced many financial ups and downs, and through it all I have continued to tithe. The sense of joy and trust in Spirit, and the sense of partnership with God that I receive when tithing, has enabled me to stay in a place of acceptance, peace, and joy despite all the challenges.

R.W.

Tithing has brought about an expansion and abundance in my consciousness and in my life in so many ways—money being the least of them. Though the money is welcomed and appreciated, it's the expansion in Spirit and my openness to experience all that life has to teach me, that I truly treasure.

K.K.

I have renewed my partnership with God. I have been tithing weekly for a couple of months. The peace of mind, the joy in participating, the joy of giving fills me beyond words. It's hard to describe my inner experience with tithing. It's as if something inside of me is relaxing and opening with and around money. I want to get down on my knees and thank God that I am giving and can give. There is so much for which to be thankful. In tithing, I feel as if I am taking my place with God and fully participating.

J.S.

When I am not tithing, miracles don't happen as often and financial concerns are more persistent. I also feel contracted. When I tithe, the partnership with God allows for a sense of free-flowing energy with regard to finances. I choose to tithe because it is so uplifting and expansive for me.

L.D.

Tithing has made me more aware of my relationship with God. I come into more joy as I write my tithing check. My day is bigger and brighter, my consciousness clearer, and my love more present.

J.L.

Tithing has been very good to me! It's often a process to write that tithing check. I always come back to the knowing that I need to be in the flow of God's abundance. So, regardless of how challenged I feel to part with my income, tithing is what I do. I want to, and need to, live within God's grace and tithing is a big part of that.

M.D.

What can I do for God, for all the riches and abundance he has given me? How can I strengthen my connection, my relationship with Spirit? Tithing is the answer to both questions. When I awakened to the spiritual warrior within me, I knew that tithing to the Traveler was a big key for me. I am grateful to give, and in the process release and let go and fulfill my covenant with God. Thank you.

K.F.R.

9/11 happened 6 blocks from my office. I was impacted financially, but I decided to continue tithing. The Light energy was very present in my office, and I found I was handling things with ease. I received money from insurance coverage I never knew I had, and new patients started to come in while old patients began treatments they had put off. Most importantly, I allowed myself to trust that God was My Partner, and that has been abundantly apparent.

D.K.

Tithing is second nature to me. I don't consciously ask myself if I am taking a breath of air. I cannot live without air. My

Tithing is something you give
unconditionally, and once you let go,
it's like cutting the string of a kite. It's gone.

But this kite flies high and
eventually reaches God's attention,
and in God's attention all the goodness
that you want will start coming your way,
like health and wealth and happiness
and more good things than I could
ever imagine to tell you.

consciousness of bounty, grace, health, loving, and abundance needs tithing in order to flourish. Also, I know of no other way to so affirmatively declare to my consciousness that I am open to receive of God's grace than to seed.

P.B.

Many years ago, even though I was in a downward spiral, I continued tithing, more out of habit than anything else. Now, looking back, I recognize that tithing was what kept me connected to God during those bleak times. I wasn't aware of it at the time, but that habitual expression of trust in God is what pulled me though the dark hours and has led me to a place of awareness of all the riches in my life.

C.W.

Since I started tithing, I have noticed that more and more of the time I am joyful. It's been a great affirmation of my partnership with God. I am always grateful for the opportunity to give back to God freely and with gratitude.

M.E.

Tithing has been the smartest investment that I have ever made. The return is so much better than I ever thought it would be. Since God is the Source of all things, I want to make sure that my books are balanced with the Big Boss and that the doors of His storehouses are always open to me. When I didn't tithe it was ignorance and foolishness on my part—I've gotten smarter now. I tithe.

S.F.

I have been tithing for many years, and each time I sit down to write my check, I take a moment to look at all I have been given, both inwardly and in the world. I don't write the check until I connect with my gratitude and feel it flowing inside of me. When I write the check, it is a physical demonstration of praising God for the gifts in my life. It is a way for me to rejoice in my abundance.

L.B.

In the moment I am writing my tithing check, I find myself lifted above my material concerns and in a place of joy. The process of tithing accesses God's energy for me, putting all else in perspective. I love to tithe.

M.A.

Tithing for me is a trust that I am given what is needed to take care of myself. It is a way for me to be consistent with that trust and with my devotion for the Lord. It is also an act of gratitude for all that is in my life.

H.B.

Tithing demonstrates directly and dramatically to me that God is my Partner and that God is personally involved in my moment-to-moment, day-to-day life—completely loving and caring for me so that my quest and my question becomes clear: How can I serve the Beloved?

L.B.F.

My experience with seeding and tithing has been incredible. I have tithed for almost 19 years and have seen my wealth, both physically and spiritually, expand every year. Seeding was difficult at first because I wanted big things and didn't know how much to seed. So I started seeding with a set amount per month for me and my family's health, wealth, happiness, abundance, prosperity, riches, loving, caring, and sharing. That's when miracles and dreams started coming true.

R.P.

My husband and I started tithing a number of years ago and often struggled to make it work, sometimes even tithing on credit. A few years ago we received a gift which has made our life much easier. I attribute this to tithing.

L.W.

Tithing for me is such a pleasure and joy, I can hardly wait to get my paycheck so I can write my tithing check. I have amazement

God is intention.

When you tithe you make God your abundant focus.

God's intention is in that focus,

so God will know right where to find you.

and surprise at the multiple ways the Lord is partnering with me and the way the grace and blessings increase as time goes on. I have more loving in my life that goes beyond my wildest dreams. My heart's desires have been met and then far beyond.

O.S.

I started tithing four years ago as a direct result of the tithing cards and tithing video. When I don't tithe right away when I receive my income, it creates problems because my mind finds all sorts of reasons not to tithe. That definitely doesn't work for me. When I do tithe right away, things work much better in my life—better ways, better times, and more ease and grace.

G.W.B.

After four years of "reasons" for not tithing, I have even more "reasons." So here's a check.

M.J.

Since you explained about tithing, I have had wonderful experiences that go beyond my dreams. People now give me a lot of things—money, clothes, and MSIA workshops. It was hard at first because I was tight money-wise. But now I am getting a lot of freedom in money matters. I am able to make ends meet a lot easier, and I know I am going out of debt. I thought it would be nice to share with you how wonderful it is to tithe.

L.P.

When I started tithing it seemed like a big risk to me. When I realized I had nothing to lose, I wrote to MSIA and asked them to send me whatever I needed to begin to tithe. I received a tithing commitment form that I signed and to this day, I re-sign that form every year. I feel this is a big key to the commitment of tithing. I sent in my first tithe, 10 percent of what I made that month. I've always held true to the 10 percent concept that is indicated in the Bible. There seems to be something very significant about this 10 percent concept that comes from inside.

Within the first week, I had my first tithing experience. It was amazing. When beginning to tithe and having one of these small miracles take place, I believe that, by giving the credit to tithing, an even greater channel is opened. I think that if I would have denied this small miracle as a coincidence, the channels would not have opened as quickly. This has been my experience. The way I show my gratitude is in a fun way. I thank what I call the "Inner Forces of Tithing."

Even though, in the time I have been tithing, my income has quadrupled, to me even more important than the things that happen outwardly are the subtle inner blessings of tithing. One of these is that there seems to be in me an ease with money and things of a financial nature that has settled into my consciousness. The way I like to describe it is that my life became more elegant, with a precision and polish to it. I look at things differently. For example, prior to becoming a tither, I used to cringe when I opened my utility bills and berated the companies as wasteful and negligent. After tithing, it became a joy to pay the bills, and I was grateful for the service I was receiving and what a good deal it was to be able to turn on the lights and listen to music. This was a great blessing to me and carried over into many other areas as well. So it has transformed my attitude, where before I was struggling with it.

It seems to me that people feel that they should try tithing and sometimes they stick their toe in, but they don't take it on as a way of life. My sense is that we are not trying it, but it's trying us, and we need to participate fully. I find that people who go into it with the expectation of getting something out of it are missing the point. The point is about joyful giving. That's the blessing.

J.H.

I love tithing. It's my favorite thing to do. It may seem a little strange to some folks, but I find it one of the easiest things to do and one of the easiest of my spiritual practices. I find handling my 10 percent physical level well to be very challenging sometimes. But tithing? Easy—just write a check each month, and I'm demonstrating to God that I love Him and that He comes first in my life.

As far as needing the money or missing the money? I don't even notice. Why? Because I truly do not consider it mine in the first place.

As to the benefits I receive back from tithing? I don't really care. That's not why I do it. I do it because I want to hold God's hand close and tight.

Thank you, God, for being my partner and letting me be yours!

K.G.

Tithing is more than a myth, and it's not true that somebody will become rich with it. Tithing is a lifestyle, in which God is always placed first, so that God places you first.

A.F.S.

Tithing should be one of the
most joyful things you can do—
to give to a Source that is reflective
of your own Source.

Your own Source then knows and understands
the vessel by which it is going to give
and receive in the world,
and it will magnify the glory
of your own countenance.

Do you want to miss that?

I don't know how many different ways seeding works,

but I do know this:

You have to seed enough to make it happen.

It's like taking wheat in your hand

and going out into the field that has been plowed.

If you throw one handful of seed,

you'll get something,

but you may not get close to what you wanted.

So you have to seed enough to make it worthwhile.

It's between you and God.

SEEDING

Seeding is a spiritual action

because God is your partner.

Seeding is planting the crop.

Tithing is saying "thank you" when the harvest is in.

Tithing and Seeding are a physical affirmation

of both abundance and gratitude.

8

THE DIFFERENCE
BETWEEN SEEDING AND TITHING

I am going to suggest an ancient idea to you that is for personal abundance. We could call it casting, "faithing," or seeding. Let me tell you how it works, especially in contrast to tithing.

In a way, tithing is asking, "What is the appropriate behavior in the eyes of the Lord?" It is saying, in essence, "God, thank you for what I have received. And from what I've received, I want to give 10 percent back to you." That's like an aftereffect: After I get it, I tithe. So, a very simple way of defining tithing, without going into the financial aspects of it, is that you're saying, "I am thankful for what I have already received."

Seeding is for a future effect and is done beforehand. It works in the same sense as when you pray over your food and say, "Thank you, God, for what I am about to receive." With seeding, you are saying, "Before I receive this, I am acknowledging the presence of it."

When we seed and tithe, it's important that we pay attention to the attitude we're holding. We have to watch the thinking and the feelings and the body, because on this planet, we know that, in terms of the polarity, there's more negativity than there is the positive. That's because the Soul is so positive that it has to have a tremendous balance of the negative polarity in order for it to stay here.

The tithing process is a statement that none of these "things" on the physical level belong to any of us. If your attitude is, "I don't have money to tithe to the church," you'd probably better, because you may lose even what you have. Or, as it's stated in the Bible, *"For everyone who has will be given more, and he will have an abundance. Whoever does not have, even what he has will be taken from him"* (Matthew 25:29 NIV)

Now, we've seen people experience poverty in the midst of plenty, and their attitude is sometimes called "poverty consciousness." It's an attitude of, "I don't have enough, and there never will be enough." But listen, there is *endless* supply. Once you understand that, you are on your way to a much higher level of freedom.

One of the things that goes against seeding and tithing is hoarding. We're vital, alive human beings, and part of our existence here is loving, caring, and sharing. Hoarding goes against that. Emotionally, it is a feeling of lack; financially, it's being miserly; physically, it manifests itself as disease.

When we start to place these blocks to abundance, we are out of line with our own spiritual directive — not the church's, not the Traveler's — our own. And when we're out of that, we can tithe and seed to bring ourselves back into alignment. We can come from all sorts of different levels and still be aligned toward God. But if we say we're aligned and we're not, we can have lack taking place inside of us. This lack could be feelings of unworthiness, or it could be where we don't have something and we say, "I don't have enough money. I don't have enough education. I don't have enough love. I don't have enough relationships." There it is — mental, emotional, physical lack.

Tithing is saying, "I give to God from what I have received." Tithing is a little bit under the law, and if you do it all under the law, you're bound. But if you do it through the grace of giving to increase things for everybody, an abundant supply comes to you in many different ways.

So technically, tithing comes under the law; it comes under the Old Testament. Seeding comes under grace as a future existence, and it's one of the most profound, best-kept secrets in the Bible. It has been called faith tithing, and we could also call it pre-tithing, except it's not based upon 10 percent of what you've received; it's based upon the amount you *want* to receive, and there's no limit to how it can come in. Still another name for it is the tenfold increase. For the bigger thinkers, it's called the hundredfold increase, and for the gigantic thinkers, it's called a million fold increase.

Seeding is the idea of going to a field with wheat in your hand and casting it on the land as they did in biblical times. The implication is that there's an attitude of gratitude for having the opportunity of owning the land, seeding, and reaping. In modern times, when you're seeding for something in the future, it is not as clearly defined how that future event will be returned to you. This is in contrast to tithing, where you know exactly how it is returned because you have already received it.

Seeding says, "I know this future event will come through God's bounty." That could be money, better health, a change in job, and so on. How does God bring that to you? However God does it. And rarely does it come just exactly the way you expect it.

This idea of casting forward through seeding must include an act that commits you to it as a mental focus. You need a clear vision, a clear idea of how you want it to be, and you seed for that. Then you wait for the harvest — not in terms of sitting down but in terms of watering and fertilizing the ground so that there's something for it to grow out of. You make sure it's watered and fertilized by keeping your mind on what you want; you water and fertilize it out of your mental desires. It's an attitude or vision.

More simply said, seeding is the planting of what you want to receive, and tithing is the harvest. It's very hard for people to shake you loose from your Spirit if you've done both tithing and seeding because, in this process, God is giving to you and you're just giving back and saying, "Here, God. Here's some more." It's a phenomenal experience, but you may not know it until you try it. If you just take my word for it, you may never know. You have to do it for yourself.

Just do it if you're after the abundance and the prosperity and the harvest. When you get the harvest, you then share it through tithing, which is grace. And then you seed again with God as your partner, which is Divinity. You're recognizing the divinity of it all, the oneness of the whole thing.

Tithing educates the lower consciousness, and seeding is cooperation with the higher consciousness. Tithe for the lower self, seed for the high self, and share it out through the conscious self. Be the source of extreme abundance and overflow for everybody around you. In this way, you come back and reconnect your power with the glory of God.

In a sense of the word, seeding is fertilizer,

and tithing is what we might call fertile ground.

In other words,

if we try to grow something just in fertilizer,

there's a good chance it might burn up and die.

So we have fertile ground,

and that means we take the fertilizer and mix it in.

9

PRINCIPLES
OF SEEDING

When you enter into seeding, there are some key principles to keep in mind. If you're going to get a crop in the fall, what is the first thing you're going to have to do in the spring? Plant it. So you have to give first. You also have to know for what you're giving. If you plant rye, don't expect a horse. If you're planting wheat, don't expect rye. So to give first, there has to be a purpose for the giving, "Why am I going to do this?" And it's not an altruistic statement. It has to be a self-possessed type of statement: "I'm seeding because I want this." Then you lay out what you want.

When you seed, you need to do it with the real faith of the heart. You have to claim what you seed for, but you have to claim it in *God's* time and love. You also have to let God know that you're his "co-pilot," his partner. And although God is the "senior partner," you can't just seed and say, "I'll let God decide what to do," because God's saying to you, "You need to give me a blueprint."

If you say, "I want to reach that mountain over there," that's called imagining. But if you're doing the seeding, you start to prepare yourself *right here* to receive of the mountain. You check that the car has gas in it and that the tires have air. You check the road map to see how to get there, and the weather to see if you want to go at that time. With seeding, you must be able to see the mountain and see a way to get there. We hold clearly the inner picture of what we want, and then we seed for it. This is a fast way to personal abundance.

The idea is much like programming the universal mind. (And if you haven't heard the audio tape *Programming the Universal Mind**, it would be a good idea to listen to it.) Get what you want as detailed as you can — as tasty as you can taste it, as smelly as you can smell it. As much as you can, activate hearing, seeing, feeling, tasting, and smelling. Then activate the intuitive sense, so that you just know. And all that will start working to pull in what you want.

You can also do a collage, or "treasure map," where you take pictures of what you're seeding toward and put them on a board, or you can create an ideal scene with the creative imagination, or you can use the technique of programming the universal mind, or you can use all of them. These things are all extremely valuable.

If you have made a treasure map or collage but it didn't work for you the way you wanted it to, it's probably because you also didn't seed for the things on it. You just envisioned what you wanted, and those things are still out there in your vision and never could

Available at the MSIA Store, online at www.msia.org

show up. You have to make a path in order for them to come in, and they come in on dollars — or pesos or pounds, whatever is the medium of exchange.

If you want to seed for something intangible (for example, a relationship), you still need to put a value on it, and the only value we all can really agree upon is money, so you determine within you what that amount would be. Then you determine, again by going within, the amount to seed for the value you have placed on that intangible thing. If you want to seed for a spiritual quality, such as clarity, you have to see what clarity would be inside of you. If you think it is one thing and it's actually much higher, you may not get what you seeded for. Or you may get the higher quality because God might know the intention of your heart beyond your ability to say it.

Knowing *how* you're going to get there is not as critical as knowing *that* you're going to get there and, in that, not having any doubts, any second thoughts — nothing except the holding and the acting as though it is going to happen. This is not sitting and thinking as though it might happen, but *acting* as though it *is happening*.

You state what you want very clearly. Then you claim it as already being here, which is conditioning the consciousness. To receive, you need to act as though you have it; this is the faith statement that it is already present. You get your purpose clear, and if you get at cross-purposes with yourself, if you undermine your seeding with doubt, your seeding rots and decays. It doesn't bear good fruit.

It's very important that you do *not* tell *anyone* the goal you're seeding toward, that you are manifesting. Not your spouse, not your Siamese twin, because they can very subtly, through not seeing your vision, cast doubt upon what you've got. You'll buy their doubt as your own doubt even if you don't want to. Then when the negativity appears, they say, "See, I was right." Then you may say to yourself, "Gee, I wonder if they really are right." The god of opinion is now taking care of you and not the great abundant God. The god of opinion doesn't deliver abundance, health, and prosperity. It delivers rip down, tear down, and alienation. That's the law. The abundant God brings grace.

"As a man thinketh, in his heart he becomes." We're creators. We can create and see what we want and go for it. We can do the same thing negatively because this process of creation doesn't care what we go toward. If you get negative doubts and thoughts, the process will manifest those for you. So in undertaking seeding, you must understand that it's a real tightrope balance in terms of what you're going to keep holding in your mind. If you start getting negative pictures or thoughts about something you're seeding for, stop them immediately. Get up and walk around. Go work off the negativity with physical movement — throwing a baseball or running around the block. Then come back to what you want with a positive focus. You want to make sure you've got this thing going in the right direction all the time, and you have to watch your thoughts carefully.

There are parts of your consciousness that, if not addressed, will allow doubt to creep in. A little bit of doubt starts to grow into

The key is in the attitude.
Some people have really gotten into the
magic of how to do seeding. They do it unconditionally,
where they just feel the joy of giving and where it
really feels good that the Church has the money and
it is going to be used for a good thing.
And with that giving attitude,
they sit in what I'd call God consciousness.
Maybe not the biggest part of it,
but certainly it's in there.It's terrific to watch.
And when they reap the harvest,
that's the best deal in this life.
Some people don't reap material benefits;
they get peace of mind.
I've seen people seed in installments,
and they got what they wanted
just after they sent in the last payment.

great negativity, until what you see is negativity. And the terrible news is that the doubt is also returned, based upon the principle "as you sow, so shall you reap." Some of you people have taken that seriously enough to say, "Do you mean that what I'm getting now is what I put out a long time ago?" Exactly. "How far back?" How long have you existed? "Well, I don't know." Since you don't know, start watching what you put out *now*. It's such a key principle to say, "You can't afford the luxury of a negative thought." It's extremely important.

You might ask, "Can I seed for a hundred million dollars?" Absolutely. "Will I get it?" I don't know. Can you have that vision working so you can really see and feel it coming to you? If you can't, you probably won't be getting that.

You can seed for as many things as you can hold a clear picture of in your consciousness. You have to watch this because it's a pretty delicate balance that you're maintaining in yourself with your environment. If you get caught in the greed of it, then you get to receive of the greed, and you may not receive what you wanted. Then you live in lack: "I lack; therefore, I have greed." But if you have abundance, you don't have lack, and, therefore, you don't deal in greed. It often takes a while to transit across some of your old, habitual personality patterns, and seeding also assists you in getting free.

What do people get when they give? Sometimes, they just get the satisfaction of giving. Seeding has to give you the satisfaction of just doing it. You draw your picture and purposely design it. You tell it to God, and you release it to God. Then you go on about your business. And if you see something else you want, you seed again, and pretty soon the first one comes in and then the next. When does it come in? WHEN IT COMES IN. What if you don't get it within a certain period of time? I would say that if it doesn't start to return in about a month, look to yourself to see what happened. Maybe you need to be more patient. Maybe you need to seed again for that same thing. Go inside yourself to find out, because seeding is between you and God.

Energy follows thought. Thoughts persisted in produce the feeling in the heart and the character that we're going to be developing. So seed with the real faith of the heart. You have to claim it, but you have to claim it in *God's* time and love, which may not necessarily be yours. When you seed that way, with God as your partner, those things then take place. And the reason all this works is that you let go and give to God, joyfully and unconditionally.

Sometimes you might say,

"This seeding that I did, I haven't got the result yet."

Maybe you didn't seed enough for the value.

So you give more, called a double portion.

So you now have a double seeding on this thing you want,

and now it's more likely to be brought forward for you.

This comes not necessarily in your timing, but in God's timing,

and God is your partner in this,

knowing what you really want and supplying it.

But it has to have something on this level to grow in,

and you are the one preparing the soil by your openness,

your willingness, your joyful-giving attitude, and, above all,

your heart and your being intentioned toward God.

SEEDING
TO THE CHURCH

We've got people who have been in this church ten or fifteen years who are now millionaires from tithing. Someone recently said to me, "I would like to have more money so I can give more," so now I'm telling you about seeding.

This is the one that Jesus did. Do you want to know the occasion he did it? The multiplication of the fish and loaves is one of the greatest demonstrations of seeding. And what happened when it was all done? They had baskets full of what was left over — leftover, surplus, more than what people could eat, more than what was necessary.

We're to have abundance and prosperity, but in the past we never knew how to get it except under the law, which is "by the sweat of your brow." Seeding is under grace. We're giving it to the church and saying, "God is my unfailing supply. With God, all things are possible." What we're doing now is fulfilling the spiritual law of tithing, maintaining that, and keeping it because it's a commandment. And with seeding, we're also casting forward into the future as part of the vision of resurrection, or the re-creation.

There's no timeline on when you harvest what you seeded for because, in God, there's no time. When you seed, you are stating that the source of the harvest is *God*. You give the seeding to the church, but the church is not the one that is going to give back to you what you seeded for because we're not saying the church is God. We're saying God is God, and the church receives the seeding as the source of your spiritual teachings.

Can you give it to other places? Yes, but it may not work as well. It may work somewhat, but you have to do more to make it work. By saying, "The church is the source of my spiritual teachings, and God is my source of all," you are involved in a sacred action.

You give to the church, you keep your eye on what you're going for, and if you have to take a circuitous route to get there, it may be because what you were after was in a different place from where you thought you saw it. On this alternate route, by-products that are blessings can appear. Are they a part of the blessings of seeding? *Definitely.*

Seeding the money to the church is saying, "I give to that which inside of me I hold as God's force on earth." That's a key thing to keep remembering. Can it work if you give it to a person? Yes, if you can see that person as God, or Divinity, or as the church, it can work that way. But most of us look at a person and find fault with them. So we'd rather give to a big organization for the greater good of all, and we call that the church. Does it have to be the Church of the Movement of Spiritual Inner Awareness? No, it can be another church. But if it doesn't work, try the Church of MSIA.

I'll tell you something interesting as an example. I wanted a palomino horse, and when I started looking for it, I must have seen six or seven pictures of possible horses. A good friend of mine was seeding to the church for me to get the palomino. (At that time, I only suspected that's what he was doing; he never told me, and I wasn't going to ask.)

One day, my friend said, "I think I know where the palomino is." We looked at some new pictures and said, "That's the one." The pictures were in the forest, and a lady was riding on the horse. We called up to get it, and the owner told us she had already taken a deposit from somebody else. My friend found this hard to accept and said, "Wait a minute. Offer her more."

I said, "That's not the way this works. We're not competing with anybody." So that horse went to the other people.

My friend told me a little while later, "I seeded for that horse. That was yours." I said, "Tell me about the image you were holding." So he told me, and I said, "You never saw me on the horse on the property." He said, "No, I didn't. I just saw the horse for you."

I told him, "If it's for me, you've got to put me in the picture with the horse, and you've got to put both of us at Windermere." The next day we received a phone call about another horse, and we drove out to see it. We both looked and said, "That's the palomino." About a week later that horse was at Windermere, and I was riding it.

God is going to direct you in how to get the harvest that you have planted. Then here comes the real good news for the church. You seed to the church to get the money. You get what you want, and you tithe 10 percent of the increase. The church is going to get the seeding and the tithe, and you're going to get the bounty. That's a win — for you and for the church. And guess who the church is? All of us. The church money magnet becomes the money magnet for all of us, and the church's land becomes a money magnet for all of us, too.

You may be saying, "With tithing and seeding, the church is getting me coming and going." Right. But you're getting everything in between. And that everything in between is a tremendous amount. For example, let's say you seed $100 for a car, somebody gives you a $4,000 car, and then you tithe $400. That's giving $500 for a $4,000 car. I'd do that any day or every day.

Your relationship with God and your awareness of money and how you can relate to it and pull it to you can be either your restriction or your stepping-stone. You're called upon to make better use of your money, as well as your time, your thoughts, your feelings, and your direction.

With seeding, God is your partner, and that is the highest good that I know of. You're saying to God, "I'm giving it to this church as a way of giving it to you, and this church can use it for whatever they want to because this is the source of my spiritual teachings." If it doesn't work, talk to God, because He's the supplier. He set it up in the Bible. It's His scriptures, His word. Talk to Him.

Take the message of what I've told you here and tell it to other people. The more people who are sowing for the harvest, the richer the valley will be. The storehouses will burst open, and a lot of people will benefit from what we're doing.

Seeding has to have a value from inside of you

placed upon what you are seeding for.

If you are seeding for world peace,

your first seed would probably be about $400 trillion.

If you are seeding for peace inside of you, it may be $4,

but it has to be relative to the value

of usability that you place upon it.

And try to have a picture of it

so that there's an object for Spirit to move into.

GOD IS YOUR PARTNER

You have to make the seeding enough so that you aren't saying, "Well, God, here's my penny. Now give me a million dollars." Do you think that's going to happen? If the answer is no, then you know it won't happen, because you can't get it into the core of your senses to bring about a connection with it and pull it toward you. It's your karma that you're dealing with that sets it for you, and everybody's got their own karma to deal with. But when you start to have success with this, that karmic restriction on your vision starts to leave because that success feeling goes, "Wow, I can enter into the abundance of this."

There are stories where people have seeded for money and the dollars didn't come, so they said, "It doesn't work." As soon as you negate it, guess what happens. It doesn't work. If you seed $35 hoping for $35,000, is that realistic? According to Divinity, it is. According to us? I don't know. Is it realistic inside *you?* If you can't make it realistic, guess what happens. That's your karma. That's the thing that stops it.

So the next principle deals with what we might call your karma. It's karmically written that some of you are never to be billionaires. Why? It would be detrimental to your spiritual progression. It is karmically written for some of you that you are not to be murderers because that's detrimental to your spiritual progression. It's also written for some of you that you are not to have great big apartment houses all over the world because it would be detrimental to your physical well-being. You would have to travel too much to take care of it all.

Along with the karma, there's also grace, and if we do seeding under the purpose and the principle that the Divinity has set forward to us, then it's handled by Divinity. Jesus said, *"Seek ye first the kingdom of God, and his righteousness; and all these things shall be added unto you." (Matthew 6:33 KJV)* That is the greatest seeding. But few people have the kind of contact with Divinity to trust it.

So you may wonder how you can trust Divinity more. How can you trust what you can't see? Well, who wakes you in the morning? Who breathes you all night long? Who drives the car when you're busy thinking of something else? Who does all these things for you? It's that part of us that is invisible, that, somehow, is always watching and aware and recording everything that's going on. If it records everything that's going on, then it can record only good if you put good forward. Get that purpose of "good" really clear because when your purpose is good, your purpose is also God.

God is your partner. That's the key principle that you've got to keep in mind. It's not John-Roger, not this person, not that person. It's God. In dealing with God, one thing you can't hold inside of you is resentment. If you hold some resentment, all your hours of faith seeding will give you back resentment. Or, even more important, the resentment negates everything so seeding doesn't seem to work for you, and then you get to have more resentment that it didn't work for you. It's not that you were rejected; you just resent that it didn't work.

As you seed and tithe, remember money is a divine energy of exchange. Money in itself does absolutely nothing for you. What the money can purchase for you is education, opportunity, recovery from illness, an increase in your ability to perform in the world, and so on. That's what money can do for you. Money itself also has no good or evil in it. So the question is, how do you use it? To your advantage or to your disadvantage? Use everything to your advantage, which is everybody's advancement. That's the key thing to get here. And know that when you enter into seeding, you receive of the grace of God's flow and abundance, and the bounty is amazing.

It's important that you are willing to receive of the bounty, however it comes in. Sometimes you will seed for one thing and get another thing. When it comes in, you may find that even though you don't want it, you sell it to someone else, and suddenly, the next thing appears, which is what you really wanted. That first thing had to come to you, then go back out, to eventually give you what you seeded for.

Faith seeding is powerful. The faith is claiming that you will receive prior to it coming to you. Faith is also basking in gratefulness for the grace of Divinity showered on you because you have seeded. And you did it joyfully.

Check to see if God keeps his word to you. And remember that the opening through which you give is the opening through which you receive. If you just fling wide the doors, what you can get will overflow to you.

You have to remember that God is the partner here,

not me, not the Church.

You're doing this between you and God.

At MSIA, we understand that concept.

So when the seeding comes in,

we also pray with it and put Light with it.

We don't want to know what the seeding is for,

just that it is a seeding so we can pray and bless it.

SEEDING
STEP BY STEP

Here is a summary of what to do when seeding:

1. Envision what you want or what you want more of in your life. See it clearly, see the details, see yourself carrying it out or living it. It can be a material item or something non-material, such as a relationship, better health, etc.

2. You can seed for as many things as you want. However, if you are new to this, we recommend that you start with one area, so you can hold that focus and see it working.

3. Check your inner levels to make sure there is no doubt or second-guessing yourself. This is very important because seeding can work as powerfully to reinforce your doubts as it can to validate your faith. We recommend that you tell no one about what you are seeding for. After you have received it, then you can decide whether you want to tell anyone.

4. When you see it clearly, put it in the Light for the highest good and make your claim. This claiming is the most important part and is the essence of seeding. It is beautifully summed up by Jesus the Christ when he said, *"Therefore I tell you, whatever you ask for in prayer, believe that you have received it, and it will be yours."* *(Mark 11:24 NIV)*

5. Now you are ready to seed by giving money to the source of your spiritual teachings. This will be the Church of the Movement of Spiritual Inner Awareness if you are a student of the Traveler's teachings, including being a minister or initiate. The money will generally be 10 percent of what you envision coming in (a tenfold return). But if you can handle the envisioning of it, maybe your return, now or in the future, can be a hundredfold or even a thousandfold. If you are seeding for something nonmaterial, we suggest you go within to find the dollar amount that represents a seed to you.

6. The final thing is that you give joyfully and with an attitude of gratitude for the blessings that are already in your life. God is the source of your supply, and so you let go of any concerns about how you are going to get what you have seeded for. That is in God's hands, and God will bring it forward for you in his own timing and in his own way.

There are many, many people who seed for my health.

I really thank them.

They allowed Spirit and God to come in a way

that I wasn't doing it.

And it's probably doing it in ways

that I still don't know about.

I'm open to receive the seeding.

It never gets old.

It's always, "Wow!"

And that's what I'm blessed with.

13

SEEDING
FOR ANOTHER

Seeding for another is a wonderful way to share your loving with your friends, family, and loved ones, placing them and their concerns, needs, or desires into the hands of Spirit. People who have seeded for those who are "not in MSIA" have had requests for more seeds, with comments like, "Whatever it is, it works!"

You can seed for something of a general nature for a person, or you can seed for their health, the resolution of something they are going through, or something you know that they want — always for the highest good. Some people have found that it works to ask for God to send a blessing to that person with the idea that God knows what that person needs.

In addition to seeding for others, you can also ask people to seed for you, for something you want or would like assistance with. This approach has worked wonders for people who, after asking friends to seed for them, reported experiencing a "seeding miracle."

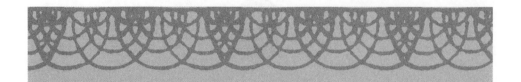

STEPS FOR SEEDING FOR ANOTHER

1. Find out the person's need, or simply seed for their highest good.

2. Send a seeding donation to MSIA, the source of your spiritual teachings, along with the name of the person you are seeding for.

3. Once you have sent the seeding donation, you do not need to hold a vision for that person; God does that.

4. It is fine to tell the person you have seeded for them; however, do not mention what the seed is for.

5. It doesn't matter if a person knows what seeding is, believes in it, or whether they know that you have done it for them. If someone tells you what their need is, they have automatically created a channel for God to be their Partner and for the seed to work in that area.

If you would like to receive gift cards for seeding for another, please contact MSIA at (323) 737-4055.

14

A Story of Seeding

Dear John-Roger,

I have a great story to tell you. It's a story about seeding.

Back around December, about the time I received the letter about seeding, I was feeling that money was very scarce. My savings were decimated, partly because I had started paying for things that my parents usually covered for me (like school fees, books, some car insurance, etc.). They could no longer afford to do so because my dad, at that time, had been unemployed for well over a year. So while I understood why my expenses had increased, there was a constant battle in my mind. I was always thinking and saying, "I am so poor," or "I can't afford this."

Then later, not wanting energy to follow those thoughts, I'd affirm abundance, but soon I'd slip back into scarcity.

I figured that $500 would replenish my savings enough to make me feel abundant again. So I seeded 10 percent on that. But even before the $500 clicked in, things started changing.

On the advice of an inner voice, I checked out an old cigar box in my mother's bedroom for U.S. Savings Bonds in my name. I found $300 worth. I blessed my grandparents and aunts and uncles who had bought the bonds when I was little, and I cashed them in the next day.

I had intended to use the money from the bonds to pay for a general fee for the spring semester at school. But by a wonderful stroke of Spirit, I wasn't charged the fee.

My best friend, who had owed me a couple hundred dollars, got a high-paying job over Christmas break and was able to pay me back.

So at that point, I felt very thankful, very abundant, and I wasn't even looking for anything more.

Then, about three weeks ago, my literature professor called me. I had submitted (in December, actually) a research paper on Emily Dickinson to an expository writing contest. He called to tell me I had won first prize — a check for $500.

It was a wonderful, wonderful surprise. I really never expected to win that contest; I've never won anything. It felt like a week-long birthday. And for the first time in many months, I bought myself some presents.

And I also thought joyously, "Seeding works! It works!" I would like to say that I knew that all along, and I suppose part of me did. But the other part of me, the one that likes hard evidence, was especially satisfied.

A lot of other wonderful things have happened to me this year. I got a car (that's another great story I can tell you sometime). And this week, my dad got a job!

R.R.

15

Questions and Answers
on Seeding

Can I tell my spouse about my seeding if we're sharing the same kind of vision?

I suggest you don't tell anybody. I've heard a lot of people say, "My husband and I, or my wife and I, we share everything." And then they proceed to share the divorce. Since God is your partner in seeding — not me, not MSIA, but God — keep it between you and God.

I don't tell anybody anything until I've received what I seeded for. And when it's done, I say, "This is what we've done." There's no way anyone can put any negativity on it, psychically interrupt it, or mess me over, because it's done.

I'm seeding all the time. I have a lot of seedings out there, but I also don't have more than what I can handle. Remember, it's not this body, nor is it your body, that's rewarding us. It is you and God and how much contact you have with God, which is where s.e.s are really important. Also important is the faith of seeing what you want coming in, seeing yourself receiving it, knowing you are going to get it. If you doubt it, the doubt goes into the seed, and you can get negative things coming forward. So this is why I say, don't tell *anybody*.

My wife and I are in a business partnership where we work together, and we want to seed together for the business because we do everything together for the business. Is that a different situation?

No, it is not. You can both seed for the business, but you don't tell each other the specifics of what you're seeding for. If you both say, "Well, let's seed for health, wealth, happiness, abundance, and more business," you can individually meditate on that. Then you send in your seeding money separately. If your spouse asks you, "What did you put into seeding?" you can say, "Darling, when it shows up, I'll show it to you." You see, it's between you and God, not between you and your partner here and God. When you seed, God is your *only* partner.

What's a good way to seed for a raise in pay?

If you want a pay increase of a thousand dollars, write it down on a piece of paper, and in the morning when you wake up, say, "I'm receiving the pay increase of a thousand dollars, and God is my partner in this." You enter into the feeling of it, the sensing of it, and then you let it go. You can do this for two days or more. And then when you have it clearly inside of you, you just let it go. At that point, it is in Divinity's hands. And when you let it go, you say, "God, it's in your hands. If I get it, you deliver it. If I don't, that seed is yours."

I know one person who did that and got fired from one job. He then went down the street to another company and got hired in the same type of position at an increased salary and with better working conditions. He also found the woman he eventually married.

I want to bring in a lot of money, but I don't have much. What should I do?

If you want a million dollars and you seed ten dollars for it, there is little practicality in that. You probably don't have enough power to attract the million dollars. A guideline is that it's a tenfold to hundredfold return on what you seed. So start from where you are, no matter how small, and build from that.

If it is a huge goal, should I seed for the huge goal or should I seed for the steps to the goal?

Why ask for a loaf of bread if you can ask for a grocery store? And a loaf of bread can be made up of many slices.

How do I seed for things that aren't material, that don't have a price tag?

Let's say you're seeding for a better relationship. I tell people to do an ideal scene of what that better relationship would be. Then

You see, this thing works so perfectly in the Spirit.
If you seeded less than what was needed to bring it to you,
the seeding will be transferred into something else
inside of you and in Spirit.

It would probably go into the karmic thing that
you need to balance, so the things you get in the future
won't be taken away through lawsuits or divorce settlements
or auto wrecks or somebody getting hurt.

So if it can be balanced-off financially
with a hundredfold return,
what an easy way to do it.

Seeding says,

"I know this future event will

come through God's bounty."

How does God bring that to you?

However God does it.

And rarely does it come just

exactly the way you expect it.

close your eyes and go inside and ask yourself, "How much is this worth to me?" And inside of you, you spontaneously come up with a figure. You now have a value statement for yourself. Then say to yourself, "How much do I need to *seed* to make my ideal scene happen?" Then inside of you, you will get another figure. And you seed that figure for that value for that better relationship.

What if I seed for something, like a relationship, that's not really for my highest good?

It won't come in. But after a certain period of time (like three to six weeks), if nothing's moving, you say, "Thanks, God, for the relationship with you," because maybe that's what the relationship was all about. God says, "I don't want you to have anybody else. I want you to have me." Well, I'd settle for that. There's no question, because God is all things, including all the *not* things.

How many things can I seed for?

You can seed for as much as you can handle in your consciousness. And you seed for each thing separately. For example, if you want to come out to Conference in July, go to Jamaica a month later, and a month after that go to northern Illinois, then you seed for all three separately. Do not put them together as one seeding because if one doesn't come off, it blocks the other ones. So you seed for them as entirely separate things.

If God's my partner, can I just seed and let him decide what to do?

No, because he's saying to you, "Give me a blueprint of what you want." Your job is to provide God with the blueprint.

Is seeding a higher law than tithing?

Seeding is not a law. Seeding is done in cooperation with the high self, so if you're *only* seeding, the lower self can feel left out. So, as I said earlier, tithe for the lower self, seed for the high self, share it out through the conscious self, and be the source of abundance and overflow for everybody around you. Somebody might come up to you and say, "Oh, my God, my kid's teeth need fixing. I need a thousand dollars." You can say, "Here's your thousand dollars. You don't have to pay me back. Go get the kid's teeth fixed, and stop worrying about it so you can do your own seeding properly."

Regarding my money magnet, would it work to keep 10 percent of the money magnet and use 90 percent as seeding?

You can seed from the money magnet or you can tithe from the money magnet. I would seed from it because I'd be increasing my supply, my return, and I'd keep 10 percent.

When you tithe off your money magnet, you're tithing into the church magnet. When you're seeding, you're not necessarily seeding into the church magnet. You're seeding into God.

Would seeding be amplified if we as a group focused on the same thing?

Yes, but if somebody throws doubt into it, guess what happens. It's amplified doubt. That's why I keep telling you to come back and reconnect your power with the glory of God. This causes a conviction to appear inside of you that's dynamic.

You see, I love this. I've done this for years, and I've never wanted to share it with anybody because I thought, "If I share this, it might be taken away." So I seeded for the giving away, and a year or so ago, it started coming up for me to share it.

Can I teach my kids to seed?

Yes. They get an allowance, so have them seed off the allowance. Seeding also teaches great money management. Kids start to realize, "I don't want to seed money for candy. I want to save it and seed it for this great big Christmas present." So they learn how to save and prepare, and they learn how to defer, to sacrifice for greater value.

I heard that if you have any doubts or negative thoughts, the seed would go negative. That's got me scared about seeding.

If you have doubt, which can cancel the seeding, and you don't get what you wanted, you can feel like you threw your money away. Then that stops you from seeding any more because you will think that it doesn't work. So you may say, "I'm not going to seed anymore because I do it negatively." The solution is to

Show your children that tithing works.

Show them that seeding works.

Explain to them the planting of good fruits

and good intentions and let them see the harvest

as the goodness that appears inside of you.

Share with them the loving

that is God being made manifest

and abundant in you.

grow up, learn to be mature, and handle it responsibly. There's no way to do this except to really do it.

What do you do with the human part that doubts?

In MSIA we deal in positive focus as opposed to positive thinking. With positive thinking, if you have a negative thought — poof! — there goes your positive thinking. Positive focus allows for negative thoughts along the way; you're just not sidetracked by them.

It's critical that, at the time you seed, you're clear about what you are seeding for. That's your positive focus. It's important that there is no doubt present at that time because that doubt will cancel the seed. It'll put bugs in your harvest. That's why some people don't know how to work seeding. They're too interested in putting their focus into doubting.

Then, once you have seeded, if doubts come up, it's okay. Just let them go. However, don't focus on your doubts or be run by them because this will corrupt the clear inner vision, your positive focus on what you want.

It's like taking a seed of wheat and putting it in the ground and watering it. In two days you don't dig it up to see how it's growing. That kills it. You never get that seed back once you've seeded it. But after it produces the harvest, you can take part in the harvest.

It's very important that you take the harvest of the seed, or you can stop yourself from receiving the abundance —

because what you take from the harvest is more seeds to plant for another harvest. If you plant wheat in the field and it comes up, if you don't harvest it, you will have no harvest next year. So you must receive of what you are sowing.

Personally, I don't put any negativity into my seeding. I just don't do it. You've got to find out for yourself how you don't do it. In fact, you have to find out for yourself how this entire process works. I'm just giving you some of the principles. It works so many diverse ways that there's no way I could begin to tell it all to you because it's each person's blueprint of his or her own karmic path of life.

If I seed for something and I change or I say, "That's not it," or it doesn't come in, is the seed still active?

Yes, but if you doubt that you can receive it, just forget it and start a whole new seed. Go from wheat to alfalfa. Don't go for a second field of wheat, which you've already poisoned by your own negative thoughts and feelings.

How is seeding connected to faith?

When you seed for something, you act as though you already have received it, which allows a space for it to come in. That's a form of "faithing." In the Bible, there's a story of a woman who reached out and touched Jesus' garment. This was a seeding action. She said, "If I touch his garment, I will be healed." It wasn't, "I touched his garment, and now I'm healed." She said it ahead of time, as an act of faith, which is the seeding process.

The principle says you get a tenfold to hundredfold return for what you seed. Then, on what you receive back, you tithe to the church, which is saying, "I got it. And thank you, Lord, for the harvest." Now you seed again. Your tithing is not a seeding. Seeding is a different thing inside of you, where you build the strength of your own faith and convictions.

Can I seed for someone else's health?

Absolutely. You do it just the same way you seed for anything else. You see their good health, you see them with vitality, the fullness of it, and you always do it for the highest good of all concerned. You send in the money — maybe it's five cents — and then all of a sudden their fingernails may straighten out, and you know that might not have been enough money.

Good health is an intangible, so you seed the amount you feel inside. It isn't necessarily a rational approach. It's more of an irrational thought, where you say, "This much will do it." Then you wait for three to six weeks. In about three weeks something should start moving. If not, all it says to you is that you did not do enough. So you send off some more seeding. In this case, it's still part of the original seed; you just didn't give enough to start with.

If you want something really big, you might seed so much every month for twelve months, until it reaches a certain point and the thing comes in. Or maybe it comes in along with something else.

Abundance comes in a lot of shapes and forms.

So the thought you have in your mind

when you do seeding,

that's the intention that your spirit is

going to be moving upon.

To complete the karma,

God may give you something else first

before giving you what you want.

There are so many ways this can work, and I don't know all of them. But I do know that it works according to *you*. I'd be really interested to have you try it and find out. And if it works, let us know, because we'll have more information about how to live this life better.

Can I talk about the thing I've seeded for if I don't actually say that I've seeded for it?

I wouldn't mess around with that. I'd keep that thing very sacred.

Can I write down what I'm seeding for?

Absolutely. In fact I suggest that you do write it down so that you can review it for about a week. Perhaps you can review it two or three times in the morning until you don't have to review it anymore because it's there inside of you.

Does it matter whether I give the money first and then later write it down?

Send the money first because then that makes you commit to doing it. If you write it down first, it's possible that you'll never get around to getting a perfect picture. You'll say, "Well, maybe this isn't quite right. I'll work on it a little while more." Send your seeding with the general idea of what it is, because God may read the intention of the heart and produce it for you within hours.

I overheard someone talking about corporate seeding. Is there such a thing, and if so, is it the same as regular seeding?

Seeding is done by individuals; corporate seeding is done by the company. If the company is owned by one person, then the owner can simply decide what he or she wants to seed on behalf of the company, and that amount is paid out of company funds. However if the company is run by more than one person, or by a board, then it is suggested that the group of people come into consensus on what they want to seed for; however, the seeding would not be discussed with anyone outside this group. Alternatively, the owners as a group may appoint one of them to seed on behalf of the company, after they have discussed and gotten clear on the company's goals or objectives. The funds would still be paid out of the company.

Does corporate seeding work?

The directors of those companies that have seeded have reported some very good successes. One company realized that a seed had returned them hundredfold. They noticed this when they went back through their records to see why their cash flow had improved. They saw that since they had seeded, they had received three large amounts of money from unexpected sources. Another company reported that they had more business than ever before, and the personnel in their company keep getting more positive since the directors have seeded.

If my wife and I come into consensus, can we do a joint seed?

No. It's a different process from corporate seeding, unless you and your wife own a company. Remember, in corporate seeding, it is the company that seeds because it has a separate legal identity. Even though a marriage is a partnership, it does not have its own identity and, therefore, the seeding is done individually.

Grace comes to you from God, through seeding,
in so many ways — most of which you won't
even be consciously aware of.

For example, your seed may prevent negative
things from coming into you that you don't know about,
which then allows the things that you want to come forward.

God always supplies my seeding — always —
not necessarily the way I wanted it,
because it may not be real good for me
to have what I have seeded for.

Sometimes it's not what you get that's the blessing —
it's what you don't get.

16

SEEDING TESTIMONIALS

I would encourage anyone who has been contemplating tithing and seeding to take the plunge, check it out, and give it time to check you out. For me, this is not just a technique — I am committed to tithing and seeding the rest of my life. If a person makes that commitment, they earn the title of "Joyful Giver," which is a glorious thing to become. I am a joyful giver.

J.H.

My daughter came home tonight and said, "Mom, seeding works." She told me that she had seeded $5 for her intention of wealth in a PTS class. A couple of days later she entered a "pay a bill" contest on the radio. She was then told she was a finalist for the contest and to listen to the radio from 6 a.m. to 10 a.m. for the entire week to see if her name was picked as a winner. She set the alarm for 6 a.m. this morning, and at about 7 a.m. she heard her name called on the radio. She called in and won the payment of a $500 bill. She said, "Well, Mom, this makes a believer out of a skeptic."

J.S.

Since we began seeding, our money goes a long way. We can even save now and satisfy our "necessities." Coming from a concept of abundance and trust seems to be the key. At the spiritual level, our seeding has been even more incredible. Every day, working with the Light and the Traveler, we are provided with the strength and the loving we need to face the challenges that come forth.

H. and H.

After I sent in my first ever seed, I immediately started looking for that million-dollar Lotto to hit, which would bring me the answer to my seed — paying off my debts and ending my money worries forever. I did seed for other things, but always with a little uncertainty because I didn't get my first seed. Then one night I started laughing uncontrollably as I realized that my first seed had been answered quite a while ago — not the way I had pictured it, but in a far more perfect way that only God can bring forward.

I have gotten my life together and have learned more discipline and become more practical in how I handle money. More importantly, I have learned to live in a consciousness of my own blessings rather than in an envious consciousness of looking at what others have and I don't. I no longer worry about bills because they are paid as soon as they come in the mail.

How grateful I am to know that the blessings already are. And I am living proof.

K.K.

If someone is new to seeding, I highly recommend they seed for small things as a way to acquaint themselves with the process. Seeding calls on us to get clear on what we want to co-create with God. When seeding, we clarify within ourselves what we would like, always keeping in mind the highest good of all concerned. Practicing with small things can make this easier.

For successful small seeding, buy a piggy bank and start dropping in coins. Some personal favorites of mine are:

- Faith in seeding *(a great way to begin the process)*

- S.e.'s *(putting change in before s.e.'s can really kick them in)*

- Relief from pain

- Social occasions to be fun

- More humor

- Good, pleasant business meetings

- A delicious meal when eating out

- Loving *(I want more love in me right now)*

- A good night's sleep *(just before you go to bed, drop in a coin)*

L.R.

It's a funny thing about this world,

but even those people

who are most likely to get what they want

don't seed because they say that they can't afford to.

I say that they can't afford not to.

I mean, if you're that pinched

and you're feeling that contracted about money,

how is money going to get to you?

You've got to have an openness to money

or you shut down the flow.

In order to get doubt working for me (it's my ultimate test of how much I really want what I say I want), I have developed a daily choosing-back process that has been assisting me in some seeding successes. I call it "watering the seed" and for 32 consecutive days I water the seed by visualizing what I want, I see myself as having it, and I send in the additional seed money to MSIA. The key for me was to continue holding the vision of my seed manifesting — not just once with the initial planting — but for 32 consecutive days.

I don't think I could have repeated the vision each day for more than a month if what I wanted was off-track for me. During the 32 days, my worthiness and willingness to receive grew stronger than the doubt. And as what I was seeding for came alive within my consciousness, the doubt became a lie.

After the 32 days of watering the seed, although I was inwardly directed to do additional watering at various times, it was clear my role was to relax and deepen my relationship to Spirit.

The seed manifested in the perfection of God's timing and I am overflowing with gratitude and appreciation for the Traveler teaching me the keys to successful co-creation with God. Watering the seed has proven itself to me as a valuable tool to support me in manifesting my co-creations with God.

L.C.B.

I had let doubt get in the way of my seeding. It wasn't that I doubted that seeding would work; it was that I doubted whether I would do it right. I mean, you have to decide on something to seed for. Then you have to get clear on it. Then you have to decide how much to seed. Then you have to keep doubt out of it.

I didn't seed for quite a while. Then one day I had an issue that I didn't know how to handle. And in my desperation, I turned to seeding. Did I get what I seeded for? I don't remember. Really. I seeded and let it go. I let go of it so well that I honestly don't recall. And maybe that alone was worth the seeding — to release the troubling concern and the feeling of lack.

I also got rid of my hesitation to seed, because now that I'd done it, I realized that if I have the right attitude, I can't do it wrong.

L.B.

People who haven't been in the experience of tithing and seeding have no idea what they are missing and what a magical, mysterious process it is. It's not about money; it's a whole other process. A love affair develops with it. I would like to grab everybody and tell them how great this process is and that they just need to do it.

The other day someone came up to me and their life was going well and they said to me, "You taught me how to tithe." I can't tell you how good that felt to be of service in that way. It was as if my life were complete at that moment. I want to be clear that

I am not a rich man. I am a very wealthy man. Many people look for the financial return, which can be an error in approach, as the return can be much bigger than that.

J.H.

Although I tithe and have known great benefits from tithing (mostly through what seems to be spiritual gains), I had yet to see any major reversal in my "earthly" money problems/beliefs. My attitudes were very limited as to the power of God's loving and support. This has all changed since I have begun seeding.

I have learned to seed for what I want in all areas of my life. I now know that God really is my Partner and always has been! I found that I had been lazy and fruitless in my creations and had been making no effort to "hold" for those things that I really wanted for my life. I judged myself as unworthy to have good and loving things. Living in my lack was extremely painful. I didn't realize how painful until I stopped doing that "stinking thinking" and moved into God's grace by seeding.

I've seeded again since that time, and more gains have begun to be harvested from those seeds. It's not just the money that I'm gaining, but little unexpected areas of good news keep showing up, and I have a new, uplifted outlook in my life. Life doesn't seem to be so out-of-control for me. I'm no longer whining inside about how hard my life is. Now I praise God and thank Him for all that I have, and I see everything I have, or have had, as a gift from God — all of it.

The experience of seeding is much like opening the floodgates on God's love in my life. I will seed for the rest of my life. To do anything less would mark me as a fool.

S.J.S.

When I seed, in order to hold the vision on what I want, I use my sanctuary. I have a garden in my sanctuary, which I call my seeding garden. And I see each seed manifesting as a rose. Each petal of the rose represents a quality or blessing. When I seed for money, I see it on a bush in my garden, much like a money tree. In addition, I also seed daily. It's a small amount and these seeds are usually not for material things, but for qualities in my life such as aware s.e.s or good health. I see them on my rose bush and I go up to the roses and smell one of the petals and I take in the fragrance of that quality.

J.H.

WHAT'S NEXT?

It's very hard for people to shake

you loose from your spirit

if you've done both tithing and seeding.

What's Next?

If you enjoyed the content of this book, we recommend that you visit our websites, www.tithing.org and www.seeding.org, for more inspirational testimonials and information about the joyful process of giving to God unconditionally. If you would like to seed or tithe to MSIA, all you need to do is send a check or money order to the Church of the Movement of Spiritual Inner Awareness (MSIA) at the address below.

You can also seed and tithe securely online at www.seeding.org and www.tithing.org. If you intend to seed or tithe on a regular basis, we would be delighted to send you a supply of secure *God Is My Partner* envelopes. To make it even more convenient for you, these specially designed envelopes have the postage already paid.

Also available upon request is a Tithing Covenant card. Since your commitment to tithe is sacred and is only between you and God, the card is for you to keep to continually inspire you.

Feel free to call the MSIA office, or email paulkaye@msia.org if you have any further questions regarding seeding or tithing.

May you be filled to overflowing with God's blessings.

The Movement of Spiritual Inner Awareness
P.O. Box 513935
Los Angeles, California 90051-1935
(323) 737-4055

ABOUT THE AUTHOR

For over 40 years, John-Roger has traveled the world guiding people to find the Spirit within themselves, and teaching how to live a healthy, loving, peaceful, and rewarding life.

In 1968, John-Roger founded the nondenominational Church of the Movement of Spiritual Inner Awareness, through which he has shared the teachings of Soul Transcendence, which is becoming aware of oneself as a Soul and as one with God, not as a theory but as a living reality.

John-Roger has led groups of up to 150 people on Peace Awareness Trainings throughout the Middle East. His journeys have taken him to such places as the former USSR, Yugoslavia, China, Israel, Egypt, Syria, Lebanon, and throughout Africa, South America, North America, Australia, and Europe.

In the late seventies, John-Roger established Network of Wisdoms (NOW) Productions, which has recorded over 6,000 of his seminars, and also produces his nationally shown cable TV show, *That Which Is*. Besides his own show, John-Roger appears regularly on television and radio programs (he has been seen on CNN's *Larry King Live*, the *Roseanne Show*, *Politically Incorrect* and many others).

His influence extends into the educational arena, as he is the founder and Chancellor of the University of Santa Monica (USM). USM offers three Master's degrees all approved by the

State of California. He also founded and is President of the Peace Theological Seminary and College of Philosophy, which offers Master of Spiritual Science and Doctorate of Spiritual Science degrees.

John-Roger is a prolific writer, with over 40 books to his name and four Bestsellers including a #1 *New York Times* Bestseller. To keep up with his writing, he founded Mandeville Press, an independent publishing house that publishes books offering a contemporary look at ancient wisdom.

In all that he does, John-Roger encourages people to check out for themselves the information he presents, and through their own experience see how it works to bring them more abundance, joy, and loving in their lives. He has transformed the lives of many people by educating them in the wisdom of the Spiritual Heart.

For more information about John-Roger, you may also visit: www.john-roger.org.

Listen, there is endless supply.

Once you understand that, you are on your way.